CW01475739

797,885 Books

are available to read at

Forgotten Books

www.ForgottenBooks.com

Forgotten Books' App
Available for mobile, tablet & eReader

Download on the
App Store

ANDROID APP ON
Google play

Similar Books Are Available from
www.forgottenbooks.com

Beautiful Joe
An Autobiography, by Marshall Saunders

Theodore Roosevelt, an Autobiography
by Theodore Roosevelt

Napoleon
A Biographical Study, by Max Lenz

Up from Slavery
An Autobiography, by Booker T. Washington

Gotama Buddha
A Biography, Based on the Canonical Books of the Theravādin, by Kenneth J. Saunders

Plato's Biography of Socrates
by A. E. Taylor

Cicero
A Biography, by Torsten Petersson

Madam Guyon
An Autobiography, by Jeanne Marie Bouvier De La Motte Guyon

The Writings of Thomas Jefferson
by Thomas Jefferson

Thomas Skinner, M.D.
A Biographical Sketch, by John H. Clarke

Saint Thomas Aquinas of the Order of Preachers (1225-1274)
A Biographical Study of the Angelic Doctor, by Placid Conway

Recollections of the Rev. John Johnson and His Home
An Autobiography, by Susannah Johnson

Biographical Sketches in Cornwall, Vol. 1 of 3
by R. Polwhele

Autobiography of John Francis Hylan, Mayor of New York
by John Francis Hylan

The Autobiography of Benjamin Franklin
The Unmutilated and Correct Version, by Benjamin Franklin

James Mill
A Biography, by Alexander Bain

George Washington
An Historical Biography, by Horace E. Scudder

Florence Nightingale
A Biography, by Irene Cooper Willis

Marse Henry
An Autobiography, by Henry Watterson

Autobiography and Poems
by Charlotte E. Linden

e urc an e
Slum

A STUDY OF ENGLISH WESLEYAN
MISSION HALLS

By
WILLIAM HENRY CRAWFORD
President Allegheny College

New York : EATON & MAINS
Cincinnati : JENNINGS & GRAHAM

LIBRARY
MAY
29
1979
TORONTO
UNIVERSITY

Copyright, 1908, by
EATON & MAINS.

BV
2863
C8

CONTENTS

LIST OF ILLUSTRATIONS

On the one hand the city stands for all that is evil: a city that is full of devils, foul and corrupting ; and on the other hand the city stands for all that is noble, full of the glory of God and shining with a clear and brilliant light. But if we think a little more carefully we shall see that the city has in all parts of the world represented both these aspects. It has been the worst and it has been the best. Every city has been a Babylon and every city has been a New Jerusalem, and it has always been a question whether the Babylon would extirpate the New Jerusalem, or the New Jerusalem would extirpate the Babylon. It has been so in the past and it is so in the present. The greatest corruption, the greatest vice, the greatest crime are to be found in a great city. The greatest philanthropy, the greatest purity, the most aggressive noble courage are to be found in the great city. San Francisco, Saint Louis, Chicago, Cincinnati, Philadelphia, New York, Boston, and Brooklyn are full of devils, and also full of the glory of God.—*Lyman Abbott.*

PREFACE

THE chapters comprising this little volume, though not in exactly the same form, were originally published last winter in Zion's Herald. Some who read these letters expressed a wish that they might be put in more permanent shape and given a wider reading. Hence this book.

It need hardly be said that what is here presented is not in any sense an exhaustive study of English Wesleyan mission halls. A much larger volume would be required for that. The halls visited, however, are thoroughly representative, and the conditions under which the work is being done are sufficiently diverse to give a fairly comprehensive idea of the Wesleyan Forward Movement work as a whole. The writing, as will be seen, was all done on the spot except part of the last letter, which was finished on board the Oceanic during the return voyage.

W. H. C.

Meadville, Pa., July 15, 1908.

INTRODUCTION

BY REV. S. PARKES CADMAN, D.D.

I HAVE long known the work of the British Wesleyan Church in city centers, and I have watched its development from the days of James Ernest Clapham, Dr. Ebenezer Jenkins, and Hugh Price Hughes until the present moment. No man can afford to neglect the study of this operation if he seeks to serve the cause of the redemption of our cities. It is replete with valuable experiences, consecrated personalities, fine energies, and grateful results.

The Manchester Mission, conducted by my friend, the Rev. Samuel F. Collier, is the best type of city mission work in the world to-day. It has honorable rivals in London, Leeds, Edinburgh, Bradford, Liverpool, Birmingham, Belfast, and elsewhere.

President Crawford has rendered American Methodism, and indeed all Christian churches, a signal service by chronicling here the results of his trained observation. I trust that the book will be widely read and duly pondered. It is the authority for the United

CHAPTER I

Manchester and Salford Mission

I PERHAPS ought to say, first of all, that my interest in Wesleyan mission halls began in 1891, when I heard Hugh Price Hughes in Saint James's Hall, West London. One could hardly hear Hughes without being won to his cause. When I was here five years ago there was great rejoicing among Wesleyans over the glorious success of the "Million Guinea Fund" movement and the purchase of the Royal Aquarium in London, on whose site, facing Westminster Abbey, Wesleyan Methodism is building a great hall and Methodist headquarters. I had the privilege of attending a monster mass meeting in the Aquarium when ten thousand sons and daughters of John Wesley sang and shouted their thanksgiving. Mr. R. W. Perks was in the chair; there were fourteen speakers, and nearly all of them had something to say of a new era for Methodism and of the Forward Movement, of which the mission hall is one of the concrete expressions. This Aquarium meeting only increased my interest in the mission halls.

CENTRAL HALL, MANCHESTER

Since the last session of the Wesleyan Conference the impression seems to have become current in certain quarters among us that the mission hall movement is on the decline. Because of this I determined to take part of my vacation to look more carefully into the work of these halls and to inquire from men on the ground just how much was being accomplished. I came to Manchester first because nowhere has the mission hall been tested as it has here. The Central Hall of this city is the oldest of all the halls, and its superintendent, Rev. S. F. Collier, has been in charge ever since its opening in 1896. For four days now I have been looking through what Dr. F. B. Meyer has described as "this labyrinth of halls, chapels, lodging houses, and other institutions." The impression made upon me has been such that I can easily believe Dr. Maclaren is right in saying: "There is no better bit of work for Christ and man being done in England to-day." My vacation plans are all broken into. I am so amazed at what I have seen and heard that I shall devote practically my whole time here to the mission halls. The work has grown far beyond my expectations.

THE APPROACHING ANNIVERSARY

I am particularly fortunate in visiting Manchester at just this time. Central Hall is about to celebrate what its friends call its "coming of age." Big plans are on for this twenty-first anniversary, which is to be held in Free Trade Hall on Tuesday, November 19. It will be a great occasion, and the influence of it will be felt by every mission hall in England. This morning I saw the advance proof-sheets of an illustrated "Souvenir of the Progress and Present Work of the Manchester and Salford Mission," now in the hands of the printer. It will be out in a few days. This souvenir sets forth in outline what has been done in these twenty-one years. In it are a few congratulatory letters from men who know at first hand what has actually been accomplished.

CONGRATULATORY LETTERS

One is from the venerable Dr. Alexander Maclaren. I had the pleasure of shaking hands with him yesterday. What a mighty preacher he has been! God bless him! He is honored and loved in America as well as here. Last evening I heard a Congregational minister say: "Twenty-five years ago, when

I was a student here in the University, Mac was in his glory. *My, but he did preach!* We've none like him now " Dr. Maclaren's congratulatory message to Superintendent Collier I give in full:

"I always esteem it an honor and a privilege to have the opportunity of bearing my testimony to the worth of the work of the Central Hall Mission. I was at its cradle, and have rejoiced in its growth to maturity. I heartily congratulate you and all your workers on its coming of age, and hopefully anticipate greater progresses in the future. You have laid the whole city under obligations, and you have given all the churches an object lesson of the greatest value. You have always kept the evangelistic side of your work well in the foreground, and yet have set us all an example of effective social work. I would that all institutional churches would learn from the Central Hall Mission the proportion which the two parts of their operations should bear to each other. I wish for you a prosperous year, and confidently look forward to much growth and success in coming days."

The following is from Dr. J. S. Simon, president of the Conference:

"I congratulate you on the 'coming-of-age' of the mission. Your work, and the work of those associated with you, is above all human praise, but it carries with it always the thanksgiving of the myriads who have been blessed by it. I esteem it a high honor to be allowed to help, in some small measure, the Manchester and Salford Mission."

Dr. J. H. Jowett, of Birmingham, who is, perhaps, the most thoroughly representative preacher in England to-day, writes:

"What can one say about your work except what every man would be glad and ready to say? I know nothing like it in England. What has impressed me most about it is this: the free play of the Spirit of God is not hindered in the amazing multiplicity of your works. I never feel smothered among them. One is always sensible of the wind that bloweth where it listeth, and the primary aim is not lost in the means. Everything is made to tend toward the redemption of man and the building up of the saints of God. Your mission offers a fine proof to the world that pentecostal power can be employed in the most modern adaptation of the Christian ministry."

WORK OF THE MISSION PRAISED

These letters are in perfect harmony with what I have heard on all sides. They are simply generous recognition of the heroic and successful Christlike work which is being done by devoted men and women whose hearts are aflame with the "white fire" of a noble purpose. Churchmen as well as Nonconformists acknowledge the ascendency of the Wesleyans in this work, and they particularly praise Superintendent Collier and his noble band of colaborers. I called on the city editor of the Manchester Guardian the other evening, and among other questions I asked him who were the two or three most influential ministers in the city. "After Dr. Maclaren," said he, "and he has practically retired now, I should say Dean Welldon, of the cathedral, and S. F. Collier, of Central Hall." I quoted this remark later to the secretary of the Young Men's Christian Association, and he said he thought the city editor was quite right. Practically the same thing was said to me by Dr. J. Hope Moulton, of Didsbury College, the greatest authority on the Greek New Testament in England. After what I have actually seen with my own eyes of the "soul-and-body-saving work" of this mission I find

REV. S. F. COLLIER

it quite easy to believe all that these men have said. I know of no better place to study the evidences of Christianity than right here.

A FEW FIGURES

Let me give a few notable figures: There are in the mission 15 centers of work; 22 services are held every Sunday; 4,338 scholars are in the Sunday schools; 3,242 are in the Sunday afternoon meetings, and in the adult Bible classes and brotherhoods. Every week there are 33 prayer meetings, 9 Bible classes, 49 open-air services, and 21 lodging-house services. Over 41,000 persons, destitute or in special difficulty, were interviewed, advised, and helped this last year in connection with the social work, and 27,986 destitute men were fed on Sundays. Four Homes and Refuges, with labor yards and workrooms, are maintained, and 220 cripples have had their lives brightened by the Cripples' Guild and the industrial classes. The field for these activities is Manchester and Salford, with a population of 1,000,000.

THE CRIPPLES' GUILD

My tour of inspection began on Friday afternoon, when I was shown through the Central Hall building. This building is a

fifty to one hundred letters are written m an evening. Many of them are letters applying for work; some are letters home. Often they talk to Sister Marion about them. When I got to the room the letter-writing was nearly done, and the letters were being brought up. Some of them were beautifully addressed. There was no reason why they should not be. Last winter they had in the club a Manchester solicitor, a Birmingham dentist, and a cap-and-gown man of Cambridge – all in the club at one time, and all chopping wood together out at the Men's Home; all brought in through drink, but "trying to work their way back." I saw an English clergyman there, a man who had gone wrong. He is trying to pull himself together. Every man who comes into the club meeting must register. Thus the workers know whether a man comes more than once. Over three thousand are on the books for the past twelve months. Placards are here and there announcing that pledges may be taken. One reads: "Wanted! Workingmen to strike against drink and gambling." The second part of the evening's program consisted of gospel songs, prayer, a short address by "the gentleman from America," and a musical feature, consisting of voice, violin, and piano.

REV. HUGH PRICE HUGHES

Sister Marion, who has charge of this depart-
ment, is a sanctified genius, I am sure of it.
Her influence upon the men is such that it is
not to be wondered at that some of them
think her an angel in human form.

THE MEN'S HOME

Saturday morning I was at Central Hall at
nine o'clock to be taken to some of the Homes
where the social side of the work is at its best.
The Men's Home, an immense building cover-
ing half a square, has accommodations for 353
men—212 boarders and 141 casuals. The
casuals are the men who are only in for a
short time, often a single night. Boarders pay
sixpence per night, or three shillings a week,
for room and bed. Casuals give three and a
half hours' work for bed and three meals.
The work is done in the woodyard, where from
a hundred to a hundred and fifty men may be
seen every afternoon, or in the tinyard, where
scraps of iron and tin cans are brought in,
sorted, and prepared for market. The men
are given work in the afternoon rather than
in the morning, so they may have the morning
to look for permanent positions. More than a
hundred men have been sent out in one day
to work at which they have been able to earn

their own living. A gentleman, not of the mission, said to me: "One of the best things about Collier's mission is *the work test*. Collier stands in with the employers because he proves his men before he recommends them. He stands in with the men because he helps them to positions. Collier believes in work. He works himself, works hard, and he believes everybody else ought to work. After he has proved the men in the woodyard or the tinyard he knows what they can do, and the employers know that he knows." Twenty one thousand have been in this Home since the first of last January. The men average three nights each. Many remain only a single night. Even that one night means much to some. Others stay for weeks. A man whose face had attracted me in the club the night before, I found in the Home spreading bread for the casuals' dinner. He was formerly a piano-tuner. Drink and some other things did it. He is trying to work back.

Dean Welldon, who is six feet three and of immense frame, climbing the three flights of stairs to the top of the building not long ago, said, as he puffed for breath, "My, but you need a lift [elevator] here, Collier." "That's what the men come for," was the quick reply.

REV. J. H. JOWETT

And they get the lift they come for. For many it is the lift that means beginning life over again.

The Women's Home is hardly less interesting than the Men's. A fine large building four stories high, with a well-lighted and attractive-looking restaurant, is found open twenty-four hours of every day. All sorts of cases come in here. Day or night the doors are always open. Policemen and cabmen, so the sister in charge told me, often bring in outcasts in the early hours of the morning so drunk they can hardly walk. The tablet in the dining hall tells the whole story· "This House of Shelter was built by James Scarlett, of Bowdon, to the glory of God and as a memorial of his beloved wife, Elizabeth Catherine Scarlett, whose tender heart was full of compassion for the homeless and friendless."

THE SUNDAY PROGRAM

Sunday is the great harvest day. I missed the morning services; had the approval of "one of the staff" for it, too. I simply could not resist the temptation to hear Jowett, of Birmingham, who was to preach in Dr. Maclaren's church. Such a sermon! I did not believe there was a man in England who could preach as Jowett does. No wonder the people crowd to hear him. He is certainly a man with a message. My afternoon and evening were full. At three it was a men's meeting in Central Hall—much the same sort of a crowd I had seen at the club on Friday evening, only more than twice as many men. I would not have believed that such a looking set could be brought together in one room anywhere on the face of the earth. Faces brutal, scarred, blear-eyed, hopeless, but wistful, many of them! There they were—the sort that hell is made of. No besotted condition described by Dante could be worse. "What a parody on our civilization!" "No," said one of the workers, "what an opportunity for Christ!" The men got, free of charge, a bun and a cup of tea for coming. After the tea there followed a gospel service. All stayed. There was not a Sunday suit in the room. "It seems that even God goes back on a man when he ain't got a Sunday suit." This bitter remark is said to have been made by a poorly clad fellow who was turned away from a London church by the policeman at the door. The door of Central Hall is wide open to the man without a Sunday suit. The most remarkable thing to me was the way the men sang and listened to the sermon. The sermon was about the man out of whom the devils were cast, and the preacher showed in a striking way what the crowd did for the man, what the devil did, and what Christ did. After the service some signed the pledge, and several remained as inquirers. I said to Mr. Fuller, one of the staff, "How much do you get out of this?" He said, "About fifteen per cent." It seemed to me wonderfully big returns out of such material as that.

WITH THE BAND TO FREE TRADE HALL

At five I was over in Salford to see a new institutional church just being opened by the Congregationalists. Sylvester Horne was preaching. At six I was out with one of the bands and helping to place ten thousand invitations to the evening meeting in Free Trade Hall, the great hall made famous by Cobden and Bright. For full three quarters of an hour the band threaded the streets within a radius of half a mile of the hall. One of the greatest fires seen in Manchester for years was raging only a few squares away. Not much of a crowd to-night, I thought. To my utter surprise, when we got to the hall nearly every seat was taken.

THE EVENING SERVICE

A chorus of fifty voices, with the assistance of the great organ and an orchestra of eighteen pieces, led the singing, which was hearty and worshipful. An exceptionally fine quartet, the Minnesingers, sang two selections of the kind to win men to a better life. One of them was Stebbins's "Launch Away." The prayer offered by the preacher was the prayer of a man who had been living in Manchester all the week and knew the city's needs. The announcements gave one some idea of the magnitude of the work carried on. The one of greatest interest to me was that next Sunday, October 27, would be the twenty-first anniversary of the opening of Central Hall, "the first hall of the Methodist Church or of any church." "When I came to Manchester a young chap of thirty," said Mr. Collier, "the most hopeful man I found was a woman. She thought we might get five hundred people. My first sermon here I preached to forty-two people. To-day my colleagues and I are preaching to sixteen thousand. Every week our visitors are reaching forty-four thousand people in this city. But our work has only fairly begun. We expect to see this city won over to Christ. There's a lot to do yet, and

CENTRAL HALL PRIZE BAND
One of six bands maintained by the mission

we're going to need all our friends to help us. So get ready for the anniversary." Then followed the collection. Thirty of the men passing the boxes were reclaimed drunkards! The mission uses its own product. There are more than twenty-five hundred such in the mission. After the collection came the sermon, which was clear, forcible, earnest, and inspiring, at some points thrilling. It was Children's Day, or Decision Day, as we call it. Earnest appeal was made for the children, particularly for "the children in the hospitals," "the crippled children," "the children half damned in their birth and training." Here are a few of the short, sharp sentences: "The hope of humanity rests with the children." "A neglected child is a scandal to the nation." "We've got to do more for the children—stand by men for Parliament who will do more for them." "How can men be devils enough to defile boys and girls?" "Do you know the place where your lad works?" "The men who lead a boy to drink deserve a 'cat-o'-nine-tails,' and I'd like to be one to give it to them." "Don't let the leprosy of your sin pollute young life." "Every boy who swears heard his first oath from somebody. Was it you?" "Where you work is the atmosphere pure, or does the foul jest come out?" There was nothing but the closest attention on the part of the audience during the entire sermon, and I did not wonder at it. In the after-service Mr. Collier said to me, "That fire robbed me of my raw material to-night." Though the number in the after-meeting was smaller than usual, the service was earnest and persuasive. Several went into the anteroom, where workers prayed with them and pointed them to Christ. I went with Mr. Collier to an "At Home" for homeless young people over on Oxford Street, and then bade him good-night and came to my hotel.

AN HOUR IN THE OFFICE

This morning I had an hour with Mr. Collier in his office—an hour I shall not soon forget. The man is altogether unconventional, yet is never undignified. He is well built physically, and seems to be capable of an unlimited amount of hard work. I said to him as I came in, "Well, is this blue Monday?" "No," said he, "I never have any blue Mondays. I have a cure." "Many would be glad to have your recipe," said I. "Begin work earlier on Monday. That's a sure cure." Mr. Collier is a graduate of Didsbury College, and is evidently a student, or he could not preach as he does. No living man could hold that great audience of three thousand people in Free Trade Hall, Sunday after Sunday for nearly twenty years, without study. I asked him if he got any time to read. "O, yes," said he, "I read for an hour and a half last night after I got home, and I read for three quarters of an hour this morning before coming to the office." S. F. Collier is a born leader, a genius as an organizer, a lovable nature, and his dominant passion seems to be to save men—not the souls of men only, but *men*. He told me of the new Hall and Institute that is to be erected on Peter Street, near the Free Trade Hall. "When we get that"—and how his face lighted up as he said it!—"when we get that, we shall have a proper home for our work. And it's going to come, too; there's no doubt about it." The anniversary gift asked for this year is $25,000—$15,000 to make up the deficit, and $10,000 for the new building, to which $120,000 has already been subscribed. The total cost of the new building will be $250,000. While in the office I was told of some of the work done by Gipsy Smith during the years he was evangelist for this mission. I saw in the morning mail what especially pleased me as a college president—many checks, some of them good-sized, too, for the anniversary and the new building.

Leaving the office, I ran out to Didsbury College for a couple of hours, and then returned to my hotel to write this letter. It poorly represents what I have seen, but I send it on with the hope that something of the new vision of possibility for the redemption of the city which has come to me may through it help somebody else. If I could have the ear of all my brother ministers in America who are expecting to visit England in the near future, I should say: Leave Durham, York, and Lincoln out of your itinerary, or even pass by Windsor, Oxford, and Stratford-on-Avon, rather than miss spending a few days, including a Sunday, in Manchester with S. F. Collier and his heroic helpers, who are winning the slums of this city to Jesus Christ. If you will see the work as I have seen it, you will feel as I do—you can't help it. Miracles are happening here. The work itself is a miracle.

CENTRAL MISSION HALL, LIVERPOOL

CHAPTER II

Central Hall, Liverpool

"You must see the Central Hall in Liverpool. The work there is simply terrific. And don't fail to attend one of their popular concerts on Saturday night." This was said to me yesterday in Glasgow by Rev. William Lindsay, son of the great Professor Lindsay, to whom I had been introduced by Dr. George Adam Smith as the greatest authority of the United Free Church of Scotland on the work of institutional churches. "He knows more about the institutional church," said Dr. Smith, "than the whole of us put together."

Mr. Lindsay has charge of an institutional church in Glasgow—the first and as yet the only one established by the Free Church. I had nearly an hour with him, and found him to be thoroughly familiar with the work of the Wesleyan halls. He seemed to know about all of them, and spoke of their work as one having authority. When he found that I had visited the halls in both Manchester and Liverpool, he could hardly say enough about the work of these two centers. He had spent unable to get in. The pitiable thing about it was that many of that five hundred were workingmen, who could not get there earlier. As I looked at them I began to see more clearly the meaning of what the superintendent, Rev. Joseph Jackson, had said to me two days before: "These concerts are to get hold of the laboring men and the men in the street who never go to church." He told me of a gentleman who came to him recently, and said: "Mr. Jackson, I was at the concert last Saturday night, and I didn't quite like it. Do you think it is the place- a Christian ought to go?" "Of course not," said Mr. Jackson, "it is not *for* Christians—it is for the men who don't go to church. *You* ought to have been at a prayer meeting or a class meeting somewhere. Besides, you did a positive wrong in going, for you occupied a seat that I wanted badly for a poor workingman who was shut out."

THE PROGRAM

These Saturday night concerts—and they are practically the same in all the Wesleyan mission halls—consist of choruses, quartets, vocal and instrumental solos, humorous readings, and moving pictures—"animated" pic-

REV. JOSEPH JACKSON

tures, they are called here, or cinematograph pictures. Care is taken to secure good talent, professional people for the most part. There are no reserved seats in the Liverpool hall, and the admission fee, including program, is twopence. Better-to-do and worse-to-do people all pay the same admission. Even at this admission fee the concerts pay. The net profit is from thirty to forty dollars per night. The mission owns and operates its own cinematograph, so that the only cost for the moving pictures is the rent of the films.

The audience having gathered, the concert began ten minutes before the appointed hour, Mr. Jackson in the chair. Nothing is done over here without having somebody in the chair. The opening number was an illustrated hymn thrown upon the screen, the audience standing and singing. My, but they did sing! The hymn was, "Let the lower lights be burning," each stanza with a different view on the screen—a lighthouse, water, and rocks showing in each, with lifeboat in last; but the same view for the chorus—and how they did sing out the words, "You may rescue, you may save"! Then followed a prayer, which was simple, earnest, direct, and short. The musical attractions for the evening were the

instructive was one which lasted for nearly fifteen minutes. It showed the process of tunny fishing off the coast of Sicily—drawing up the nets, putting the fish on ship, the return, unloading a colossal catch of two hundred thousand pounds, cleaning and cooking the fish, putting them in cans, and extracting the oil. Nothing in all the program pleased the people more than the moving pictures. During the interval between the first and second part of the program Mr. Jackson announced the events for the week. It was a full program, too—Sunday services, class meetings, brotherhood and guild meetings, and another concert in one week. Announcement was also made of the approaching anniversary, on November 26, when £2,000 would be asked for, for the double purpose of paying off the debt and carrying on the work. At the beginning of the second part of the program, and again at the close, there were illustrated hymns—"O! what a Saviour," and "Onward, Christian soldiers." The people of Manchester and Liverpool certainly know how to sing, and they do it so heartily. It did my soul good to hear them. The concert closed at just five minutes past ten, having lasted two hours and forty-five minutes; but not a

REV. CHARLES GARRETT

"Pledge King." He has secured fifty thousand signers.

CENTRAL HALL AND CHARLES GARRETT

Mr. Jackson seems to be a man well adapted to his work—sees what is to be done and does it. He is a graduate of Headingley College, and had four years with Peter Thompson in the East London Mission. He was with Josiah Nix, secretary of Race Course Mission, and was the first secretary to the British Chautauqua. He has been in his present position for eight years. Mr. Jackson is peculiarly fortunate in his building—Central Hall. It is new—has only been in use for two years. It was built at a cost of $250,000. There is still a debt of some $40,000, but it is so arranged that it will be gradually paid off at anniversaries. Central Hall was built as a memorial to Rev. Charles Garrett, the founder of the mission and a man whose name is still almost a household word in Liverpool—one of those rare men who bless any city. His is one of the names known in all Methodism. On the right hand in the great entrance hallway is a bronze tablet, reminding all who pass that the hall is a "Memorial to Rev. Charles Garrett," and that the Central Hall buildings

SAINT GEORGE'S MISSION HALL, LIVERPOOL

renders valuable service. Many a man is brought into the Sunday evening meeting through the band. I asked a newsboy in Saint George's Hall Square if he could tell me where the Central Hall band played on Sunday. "Yes, mister," said he. "They play just there in front of the steps. They play every Sunday afternoon. If you will come to-morrow afternoon at four o'clock you will hear them."

NUMBERS INCREASING

The number of communicants in the mission is growing rapidly; but the mission is not getting its congregation from other places of worship. The chairman of the district said, not long ago: "This is a *new* Methodist congregation gathered from the streets." Some dockers were overheard to say they could not recall when they went to a place of worship before the Central Hall was built "I have not been in a hall or chapel since I was wedded," said one. A worker in the mission heard two young men, outside the Hall, one Saturday evening, arguing whether it should be the Empire Music Hall or the Central Hall. (The Empire is a large variety theater.) Finding it difficult to decide, one of them said,

INTERIOR OF CENTRAL HALL EDINBURGH

CHAPTER III

CENTRAL HALL, EDINBURGH

WHEN in Edinburgh five years ago I said to our hostess, one Saturday evening: "To-morrow will be our first Sunday in your city. Where shall we attend church?" After asking what church we attended at home, and finding out that we were Methodists, the good lady said: "Ah, well, then, you must hear Dinsdale Young in Wesley Chapel in the morning, and you'll not hear better in Edinburgh. Then, if you like, I should be glad if you would hear our minister, Hugh Black, in Free Saint George's in the evening." George Jackson was at that time in the height of his popularity at the new Central Hall in the West End, almost under the shadow of Castle Hill. All three men are now gone from Edinburgh. Young is at City Road, London; Black is in New York city; and Jackson is in Toronto. These three men wielded great influence from the pulpits they occupied. They were quite different in their type of preaching—Young, expository and eloquent; Black, with a touch of the mystic in him, poetic and spiritual;

Jackson, keen, incisive, persistently enthusiastic, his words contagious for good, impressing profoundly all who heard him.

BEGINNING AND GROWTH

The history of Central Hall is little else than romance. It is what one likes to read about and hear. It makes one feel that the heroes and prophets are not all dead. The hero of Central Hall, Edinburgh, is Rev. George Jackson. He came to this city in the year 1888 to be pastor of the Wesleyan Methodist Church in Nicolson Square. Mr. Jackson had not occupied the pulpit in Nicolson Square many months before he became inspired with the idea of founding another Wesleyan Methodist church in this city. He was deeply impressed—as many others have been—by the many thousands of persons who rarely, if ever, enter a place of worship, and he felt that, notwithstanding the predominant position held by the Presbyterians, Methodism had a place and work where such conditions existed. The original aim of Mr. Jackson and those who rallied around him was to gather a congregation and build a church, which, in his own words, "would do for the Methodists on the west side of the

REV. GEORGE JACKSON

city what Nicolson Square Church was already doing on the east side." The movement, when it started, was known as the "West End Mission," but circumstances gradually led to its occupying a remarkable and commanding position, which it has now held for some time.

BOLD MOVE FORWARD

In starting the movement Mr. Jackson was ably assisted by a few energetic members of the Nicolson Square congregation. The Albert Hall in Shandwick Place, a few doors to the east of Saint George's Free Church, was selected as a meeting place. The building, which was then used as a second or third rate place of entertainment, was rented at first for Sundays only, the opening service being held in November, 1888. For the first few months the attendance was small, but ere long there were evident signs of real progress. In June, 1890, a bold step was taken, when Synod Hall in Castle Terrace was engaged for the Sunday evening services. The hall, which is one of the largest in the city, holds about two thousand persons, and there were many who thought Mr. Jackson's venture in entering this hall was far from judicious, the mission at that time being only two years old. But the wisdom of the step was soon apparent to all. In a remarkably short time "Mr. Jackson's Synod Hall Meeting" (as it was called) became one of the Sunday evening institutions of Edinburgh. Week after week the hall was filled to overflowing; and from year to year the "meeting" continued to maintain its popularity—one of the most notable features, perhaps, being the large number of young people who attended. The growth in the actual communicant membership of the mission increased by years, as follows: In 1889 it was 50; by the following year it had increased to 100; in 1891 it rose to 201; in 1892 it was 290; and by 1893 it had reached 357. Since then, and up to the time of the building of Central Hall, it increased steadily until it reached nearly a thousand.

Almost from the very beginning this mission seemed to have the good will of the community. This was due in large measure, if not altogether, to the personality and attitude of Mr. Jackson. From the outset he deprecated the idea of the mission being in any way antagonistic to other religious bodies. "We are not here to make Presbyterians into Methodists," he said. "From the first day of our existence we have set our faces like flint against proselyting in any form. Christ's army is not any the stronger merely because one hundred of his soldiers are persuaded to change their regiment, although, of course, there may be individual cases in which the change is an advantage all round. I often tell my people that if ever a day should come (which God in his mercy forbid!) when all that we can do is to lead saints to change their *ism*, and not sinners to change their lives, they will have to look out for a new superintendent." These and similar broad-minded declarations were warmly reciprocated by leading Presbyterians, ministers and laymen alike. Many gave Mr. Jackson a hearty Godspeed and substantial assistance in a variety of ways. Among the ministers who coöperated with him may be named Dr. Alexander Whyte, Professor Marcus Dods, Dr. John Watson, Dr. George Matheson, Dr. Stalker, and Dr. Denney.

Mr. Jackson did much to increase his popularity and influence here by his writings. His book First Things First, which has passed through several editions, was warmly received by the people of Edinburgh. This book is a collection of addresses to young men. It offers good opportunity for insight into Mr.

Jackson's methods of thought as well as his
style. It displays something of the gifts
which gave him such meed of popularity here
in the Scottish capital. All his discourses had
a manly ring about them. Without being
sensational, or going out of his way to make
himself singular, he was entirely unconventional. He is a man of high ideals, and great
earnestness distinguishes all his efforts. Without being an orator in the ordinary sense, he
is a highly effective speaker; his style is terse
rather than grandiloquent, and incisive rather
than rhetorical.

It was through the ability, zeal, and or-
ganizing skill of Rev. George Jackson that
Central Hall was built and finally opened in
October, 1901. When the question of the
building was first mooted, it was suggested
that an adequate mission house could be
erected at a cost not exceeding $75,000. At
that time a scheme so bold as what was even-
tually adopted was not even dreamed of.
But the size of the congregation, together
with the magnificent opportunity, led Mr.
Jackson to push his way toward the final
erection of Central Hall, which cost $250,000.
It has an audience room which will accom-
modate two thousand people, and is admirably

adapted in all ways to the purpose of the mission. There is still a debt—rather a large one —but, with the rental of the stores underneath and the proceeds of the anniversaries, the debt is in such shape as not to be a burden. For many of the above facts I am indebted to a very comprehensive article which appeared in the British Monthly of October, 1901, written shortly before the opening of the hall.

EXPRESSIONS OF GOOD WILL

It is not too much to say that all the promises for the success of Central Hall made at its opening have been fulfilled. Mr. Jackson was with the mission for five years after the opening of the new building. His popularity and influence continued to increase up to the time he left. Much joy has been expressed because of a recent announcement in the Methodist Recorder, that after two years more in Toronto, Mr. Jackson will return to England. Where his work will be is not now known, but good opportunities will open to him.

The thing that most impresses me here is that the mission is totally different from what I saw in Manchester and Liverpool. In fact, it is not a mission at all, in the sense of emphasizing rescue work. It is simply a great people's church, quite similar in character to Spurgeon's Tabernacle in London. Of course, constant appeal is being made to men to surrender their lives to Jesus Christ, but the mission is not in touch with the slum. One of the stewards said, in reply to a question: "O, yes, Mr. Jackson did try once to get in some of the slum people. They came to one service, but they did not come again—at least not many of them." Another steward said: "You would hardly expect slum people to come here. These are respectable folk who come to Central Hall." Yet, in its way, Central Hall is doing a remarkable work for the common people—the artisan class, the fairly well-to-do working people. The venerable Dr. Alexander Whyte said to me: "Yes, it's a great work they are doing in Central Hall. We all look with favor upon it." Dr. John Kelman, successor to Hugh Black, whom I heard with great delight on Sunday morning —a man of rare preaching power, in fact, the most popular preacher in Edinburgh to-day— said, when asked what Central Hall was doing that the churches could not do: "It is doing a great deal. There is a freedom and a brotherhood about it which the people like It reaches them in large numbers. George Jackson is a remarkable man. I believe in him down to his boots, and the present superintendent is carrying on the work well." Professor Paterson, whom I had the pleasure of meeting at Des Moines, Iowa, a year ago last May, when he was attending the Presbyterian General Assembly as fraternal representative from the Scottish Kirk, said to me last evening that Mr. Jackson's work in Central Hall was a real contribution to the Christian work of the city. He felt there could not be too much work of that kind. From all classes of people I have heard only good words for Central Hall. It has the confidence of the community to a remarkable degree, but it is not doing rescue work, as it is understood in the London missions and in Manchester and Liverpool. In fact, the only church that is doing anything of that sort here is the Established Church of Scotland. I was in one of their Homes last evening, and was greatly delighted with what I saw. A little rescue work has been done by the Church Army of the English Church; and, of course, the Salvation Army here, as everywhere, is going to the very lowest. I ought to say for Central

Hall that, a month ago, meetings were opened in the Alhambra Theater—a rather low variety place—under its auspices, for the purpose of reaching the slum district. The present superintendent, Rev. F. H. Benson, is very anxious about this work, but so far the venture has been a doubtful success. One of the stewards reported last evening

the meeting, and "half of them children." The slum districts exist in Edinburgh; some of them are as bad as anything to be found in East End, London; but the churches have not yet seriously grappled with the problem. This has been said to me frankly by several men of influence in this city.

I am glad to be able to report that Central Hall, under Mr. Benson, the new superintendent, who has been here now for little more than twelve months, is in the high tide of success. The mission is certainly fortunate in securing a man to succeed Mr. Jackson who seems to have just the qualities of leadership necessary to success here. Mr. Benson is a young man, thirty-four years of age, and has been out of college (Headingley) only ten years. I heard him on Sunday night, when the hall was packed. He preached from

REV. F. H. BENSON

the text, "And they left their father Zebedee in the boat." The sermon was a discrminating, strong, and forceful putting of call and responsible choice. The appeal to young men to hear the call of Jesus Christ, surrendering everything that he asked, was simply tre-

an hour, about two hundred remaining. It was a wholesome, impressive service, but nothing in it touched me so much as the prayer of a white-haired old man who, in broad Scotch, prayed "for the bairns who have gone awa' quenching the Spirit." Immediately following the after-service was a social hour in the guild room, in which perhaps a hundred young men and women, most of them living in lodging houses, sat about tables, had a cup of tea, and conversed. There was some singing, joined in by the whole company, and a solo by one of the members of the choir.

CONCERT AND MEN'S MEETING

On Friday evening I attended one of the guild meetings of the mission, which is something like one of our Epworth League services. I also attended the concert on Saturday night, which was quite unlike the one I attended in Liverpool. It was simply a high-grade con-

CENTRAL MISSION HALL, BIRMINGHAM

CHAPTER IV

LEEDS, BRADFORD, SHEFFIELD, AND BIRMINGHAM

COMING down from Edinburgh to Leeds, I found conditions much like those I had seen in Manchester and Liverpool. Leeds is the fifth city of England in point of population. It lies in the center of a richly productive agricultural and grazing region noted for its extensive coal fields. It has exceptional railroad facilities and water connection with both east and west coasts. Located not far from an old Roman station, Leeds has been an important center since the times of the Saxons. Its first charter was granted by King John, and dates from 1208. As a manufacturing city it is chiefly known as the great center of the British woolen trade. The iron industry has important place in the city's activities; there are also extensive manufactures of earthenware, leather goods, silks, paper, glass, and fire brick. It is claimed that the annual value of the Leeds products is about $60,000,000.

METHODISM IN LEEDS

Two generations ago this thriving York-shire city was fairly overflowing with Meth-odists. A vicar of the time said, "Methodism is the established church of Leeds " He was not far wrong, for in those days every seventh man was a Methodist. Right in the heart of the city and within a few minutes' walk of each other were four Wesleyan chapels, with seating capacity of two thousand each, and all filled every Sunday. Fifty years later a very different condition of things existed. The four chapels were almost deserted. The attendance of all four was not more than the attendance of one had been in the years of prosperity. Great manufactories had been built in the locality, and people of the better-to-do class had moved to the outlying dis-tricts. The chapels were in a sad state of discouragement.

The Methodists of Leeds faced the very problem we have been facing in these recent years in our larger cities. We have solved the problem in some places by selling our downtown churches and using the money to build new uptown churches. The Wesleyans determined upon another method. They turned one of the chapels—Wesley—into a

REV. C. W. ANDREWS

mission. This was seventeen years ago. Later, two others—Saint Peter's and Oxford Place— were added. The problem of Saint Peter's is still unsolved. This chapel is in the slummiest part of the city, crowded with Irish and Jewish population. At Wesley and Oxford Place the success has been most marked. Every Sunday the auditoriums at these centers are crowded to overflowing. Oxford Place is perhaps the largest of all the halls. It is the old chapel done over, but at an expense of $150,000, and presents a stately appearance even when looked at in comparison with the fine Town Hall just opposite. The growth in membership in these three missionized chapels, from 1890 to 1906, was from 301 to 1,988—a net increase of 1,687. But the growth in membership is only a slight indication of the actual work and growth of Methodism in the downtown district of Leeds. The prevailing note seventeen years ago was utter discouragement. This statement is made on the authority of representative men who know the facts. The prevailing note to-day is one of triumph. Thus in less than twenty years Wesleyan Methodists have solved the problem of the deserted chapels in the downtown district of Leeds. Of course, there is much yet to be

long to wait for the crowd. The news of his conversion spread like wildfire. It was discussed in every public house and every barber shop in the district. Hundreds came to church, not to see Jesus, but the man he had raised from the dead. A glorious revival followed, in which many were turned to God. That was my first great discovery. Lazarus solves the problem of empty churches. He is the greatest attraction and the strongest argument. Wherever there is the continual operation of saving power, bringing dead men out of their graves, the work of the Lord will prosper. For this power there is no substitute, and it never fails. There are no languishing churches where souls are saved. People believe when they see graves opened and the dead come forth in newness of life. This has been the first fundamental of my working creed." "It is no exaggeration," says Mr. Chadwick, "to say that all I know of mission work was discovered in that revival."

The second fundamental of his working creed—and he has only two—was found in a very different way. It was at Clydebank, Glasgow, a new town which had sprung up with the rapidity of one of our Western American cities because of the large industrial

DR. H. J. POPE
General Secretary Wesleyan Home
Mission Fund

works which had been planted there. The Lazarus was soon found, but the "epoch-making event," as Mr. Chadwick calls it, was a bit of temperance work which he undertook single-handed. He found that the brewers had seized the most strategic positions for public houses, and when the spring sessions came round they made application for five new licenses. Temperance workers in the community were discouraged because of previous failures, and the young missioner saw that if anything was done he must do it. The experience in the court room is best told in Mr. Chadwick's own words: "It was my first appearance in court. The proceeding was unusual, and there was a wrangle over a question of order, in which I scored. The barrister who held the brief for the applicants made great sport of me, and everybody except myself seemed to enjoy the fun; but the Lord delivered him into my hands. He wound up his banter with an attack upon me as a minister, and in mocking tones instructed me in my pastoral duties as a shepherd of the flock of Christ. It was hard to bear, but I sat still. At last he turned to me, and with withering scorn said: 'I should like to ask this young-looking shepherd, What hast thou done with the few sheep in the wilderness?' Quick as thought I sprang to my feet and flung out the answer, 'Don't you trouble about my sheep; I am after the wolf to-day' Then the laugh was on the other side, and those sedate old magistrates cheered like schoolboys. We got the wolf, but more important than the fact that for three years we prevented any new license being granted was that on my feet in that court I discovered the second working principle of a missioner's life. From that day I have regarded it as an essential part of my sacred calling to hunt the wolf as well as to care for the sheep."

It was from such training and experience, and with the feeling that outcasts are not difficult to reach when the church really wants them, that Mr. Chadwick went to Leeds in 1890, an evangelist and a social reformer who thoroughly loved to track a wolf. From the beginning, however, he emphasized the fact that conversion is the key to the problem of personal salvation and church prosperity. The transformation which came about in Wesley Chapel, Saint Peter's, and Oxford Place has already been described. For sixteen years Mr. Chadwick, who is regarded as one of the strongest preachers of the Wesleyan Church, has maintained in Leeds, at the sessions of the Conference and at mission anniversaries, that the mission of a mission is to save the lost, attack the devil, and bring in the kingdom of God. His definition of mission theology is so thoroughly pertinent that I cannot forbear giving two quotations: "An evangelistic mission implies an evangelical faith. A theology that is not missionary is of no use in a world like ours. The frozen abstractions of metaphysics are as powerless to save as the dead creeds of tradition. The speculations of theologians must be tested by their power to heal and save. Missions exist for the lost. Their work is not educational and social, but spiritual and redemptive." "Anything less than Deity is powerless to save men from sin. If Jesus be not God, he may be a great philosopher, a superb idealist, an unrivaled guide to the new order of life, but he is useless as a Saviour. Let the new theologies prove themselves in missionary campaigns among the lost. Missions have no use for a Christ that cannot save to the uttermost all who come unto him. For the same reason we hold to the complete and final authority of the Scriptures. We cannot go to the perishing with the 'perhaps' of balanced probabilities. We need the certainty of a 'Thus saith the Lord.' " Mr. Chadwick's work in Leeds is hardly surpassed by any.

My visit to Oxford Place was on one of the class-meeting nights, where from many rooms there rang out inspiring hymns and gospel songs. The present superintendent, Rev. C. W. Andrews, has recently come from a most successful work at Bolton. Oxford Chambers adjoins the chapel proper. Here are the head quarters of the Wesley Guild, which is the Epworth League of English Methodism. Headingley College, situated in an attractive suburb twenty minutes' ride from Leeds, is an institution of which English Methodism may be justly proud. Dr. Banks and Professor Findlay, distinguished and honored professors in this college, are both ardent friends of the mission halls. Dr. Banks has been chairman of the Leeds Mission from the beginning, and is a strong believer in the work which is being done. On leaving Leeds and thinking over what I had seen and what I had been told of the transformations which had come about in the sixteen years in these deserted chapels, it seemed a real fulfillment of the prophecy, "The desert shall rejoice, and

EASTBROOK HALL, BRADFORD

blossom as the rose. It shall blossom abund antly, and rejoice even with joy and singing."

BRADFORD MISSION

In the late afternoon I went by express train to Bradford, a thirty-minute run, where I spent three hours with Rev. H. M. Nield in Eastbrook Hall. On leaving Manchester Mr. Collier said to me: "Whatever else you do, you must go and see Nield's Brotherhood in Bradford. It is the greatest thing in England" Later, a mission worker said: "Have you been to Bradford? They have a great Brotherhood there, made by a race horse." Another said: "The success at Bradford is all due to a fortunate tip on the races." I had heard so much about the man and his methods that I was quite prepared to find Mr. Nield something of a sensationalist. He was in conference with a dozen of his associates when I arrived, which gave me ample opportunity to see the main features of the glorious hall before our interview.

EASTBROOK HALL

Eastbrook Hall is new; it was opened only three years ago. Its appearance, facing the street, is quite like a first-class music hall.

The auditorium is reached by a broad en-
trance-way, and is on the plan of the Ber-
mondsey (London) Mission Hall. There are
sittings for something over two thousand.
The room is well lighted and has a most ex-
cellent system of ventilation. The lower part
of the building faces two streets. It is devoted to shops and offices. The
are divided up into halls, classrooms, clubrooms, and rooms for the Men's Institute.
The building is a marvel when one takes into
account the cost—$150,000. It represents
more for the money than anything else I have
seen.

A TIP ON THE RACES

After taking tea with Mr. Nield and his
associates, and visiting, under his guidance,
parts of the building I had not seen, I spent
an hour with him in the vestry. When we
were alone I said, "Mr. Nield, I want you to
tell me the story of your race horse of which
I have heard so much." After some hesita-
tion he told me this story: "Some two years
and a half ago, shortly after this hall was
opened and the week before the races, I announced that I would speak on Sunday afternoon at three o'clock to men, on the subject,
'What'll Win?' We had worked up the meet-

REV. H. M. NIELD

ing pretty carefully, advertising it well, and the hall was nearly filled. In beginning my address, I said: 'Men, what are you here for? You certainly do not expect a Wesleyan parson to give you a tip on the races.' Then, pulling out of my pocket a card which had been sent to me anonymously the day before, I said: 'Evidently someone does expect me to do just that, for I have received this card, which reads: "As to your subject for Sunday afternoon on What'll Win? would say that Hackley's Pride is good for the Cambridgeshire." ' Well, there was a regular guffaw all over the house. Hackley's Pride was a fourth-rate horse which nobody expected anything of. The thing that happened was this: On the following Wednesday Hackley's Pride won the Cambridgeshire. The next Sunday afternoon Eastbrook Hall was filled long before the hour for the meeting, and hundreds were turned away. It has been full every Sunday since. Over five thousand men have joined the Brotherhood within two years and a half, and there are now actually 3,725 members. All wear a blue and gold button with the letters 'E. B.' on it."

The growth and success of this Brotherhood is certainly a triumph. It is known

throughout all England. No feature of the
mission hall work, apart from the social side
of Mr. Collier's activity, is spoken of so fre-
quently as the Brotherhood at Bradford. It
is the phenomenal success of this Brotherhood,
and of others which have sprung up because
of it, which led Mr. Perks to suggest the idea
of a federated Brotherhood for all Methodism.
After the experience of that hour in the vestry, during which I talked with Mr. Nield
concerning the character of his methods and
the nature of his appeal, I was thoroughly
convinced that there was nothing of the sensationalist about the man. He is simply a
true, brave, fearless preacher of the gospel.

A FEW FACTS

The following crisp paragraphs from the
latest report of this mission are suggestive:

"The Eastbrook Brotherhood has enrolled
over five thousand members in two and a half
years. Brotherhoods have sprung up all over
the city, but the 'E. B.' reports 3,725 members
at the present time."

"The Eastbrook Women's Meeting has enrolled over two thousand members in eighteen
months, and has to-day 1,643 members on its
registers."

"During the three years the hall has been opened, 1,184 penitents have passed through the inquiry room. The 'soul-converting power' characterizes the whole work of the mission."

"A living church has been built up. When the hall was opened Eastbrook had 334 names on its class books. It has now over a thousand. The class moneys alone last year totaled £276, 2s. 2d."

"By the open-air campaign of last summer we touched between two and three thousand souls a week."

SHEFFIELD MISSION

The work in Sheffield is in a transition state. The Sunday afternoon and Sunday evening meetings are still held in the great Albert Hall. The other activities of the mission are centered in Montgomery Hall, some two squares away. A fine new Central Hall is in process of erection on Norfolk Street, a prominent thoroughfare of the city and right in the center of the city's population.

THE WORK IN BIRMINGHAM

The stateliest and most imposing of all the mission halls is Central Hall, Birmingham, erected a few years ago at a cost of $350,000. This building is of red terra cotta. In ex-

This transformation process is going on all over England. It is made possible through the fact that the English government is just now reducing the number of public houses, in some quarters greatly reducing them. As soon as a license is withdrawn the public house is vacant. There is nothing for it to do. The property is not valuable for any other business and is usually for sale cheap. In a goodly number of instances the mission workers have seen a real opportunity in the vacant property because of its strategic location and have purchased it, transforming its uses in the manner described above. Dr. Jowett spoke to me with much enthusiasm of these transformations by which an instrument of darkness is made to be an instrument of light.

would not be too much, but, fearing that my readers may become weary, I feel that I must close the series with this letter. Perhaps I can best give some idea of the impression made upon me by summing up briefly the work and condition of each, and _____ attention to two or three distinctive and outstanding features of the work as _____ it.

Arriving in the great _____ metropolis on Saturday evening, I t_____ only to get established in my hotel, _____ ng a hurried supper, I went directly to Leysian Hall. This stately and magnificently imposing hall is on the famous City Road, and only five minutes' walk from the cathedral of Methodism and the sacred spot where lie the mortal remains of our great founder. Leysian Hall is unique. It is a mission hall and a social settlement house combined. In its founding it had in it the culture and far-reaching Christian purpose of Dr. W. F. Moulton, who inspired the boys in Leys School, Cambridge, to learn the lesson of brotherhood and "the skill to draw to light the hidden good." The other man was Hugh Price Hughes, whose counsel was sought in the selection of the first headquarters, in White Cross Street.

The spacious auditorium of the present

in character to the one I had seen in Liverpool. The entrance fee, including program, was a penny; but even at this fee the concert more than pays expenses. To me the most thrillingly interesting feature of the evening was a twelve-minute temperance address by Mr. Parsons. This was given between the first and second parts of the program. It was based upon certain facts disclosed in a series of articles appearing in the Tribune on "The Black Stain," or child mortality, by George R. Sims. There was hardly a moment when the silence was not almost oppressive as Mr. Parsons plumped facts, figures, and concrete cases at that audience. When he came to his closing sentence of appeal he was cheered to the echo.

During the evening, and again on Monday, I looked through the establishment. There is almost a bewildering labyrinth of rooms, but every room has its use. Often a room must do duty for several interests. The mission is crowded in all departments, and the departments are many. A list of the agencies which was handed me included sixty-one items—among them the Coal Club, the Thrift Club, the Penny Bank, the Lantern Services, Public House Visitation, Dinner Hour Serv-

REV. PETER THOMPSON

ices, and the Guild of Prayer. Five years ago, when I was in London, this mission was a very small affair; now it has a communicant membership of 1,887. Many homes in this part of London are touched and influenced by the gospel of social and spiritual regeneration which is here preached.

The third anniversary of the men's meeting of this mission was held the last week of October—a meeting quite like the Eastbrook Brotherhood of Bradford—and was presided over by the Lord Chief Justice, who delivered a most worthy address on the "Brotherhood of Man," in which he showed how men's meetings like the one in Leysian Hall may contribute to the realization of the highest ideals of human brotherhood. Before the anniversary closed, the Lord Chief Justice, at his own request, was admitted to membership and decorated with the button badge of the Brotherhood.

EAST LONDON MISSION

The story of Peter Thompson and his heroic work in East End has been told so often that I need not repeat it here. What a man of God he is! It is almost worth while to cross the Atlantic to grasp his strong hand

and see the flash of his keen, kindly eyes. I shall never forget the half-hour with him in the new hall of which he is so justly proud. It was no ordinary event for that part of London when, one day last summer, the Wesleyan Conference met in the glorious auditorium for the formal opening exercises. The front part of the building is not yet completed. It is hoped that it will be finished by the end of the coming summer. The cost of the whole building will be $180,000 The membership, not including juniors, is nearly two thousand. "The work of this mission," said a prominent Wesleyan, "touches bottom. It reaches the very lowest " Old Mahogany Bar and Paddy's Goose (public houses transformed into missions) will continue to render noble service, and many a man through them will go to the new hall, perhaps to a concert first, such as I saw there on Monday evening, and then to the men's meeting or to the service on Sunday evening. The building is not finished yet, but when it is all completed, and the forces of the mission thoroughly organized under the magnificent leadership of the veteran superintendent, we shall see a mighty work in progress. The "black patch" may yet become the garden of the Lord.

REV. J. GREGORY MANTLE

CENTRAL HALL, DEPTFORD

The time of my visit to the great hall at Deptford was most fortunate. It was on the first Sunday afternoon in November when the men's brotherhood, some seventeen hundred strong, were out to give their superintendent, Rev. J. Gregory Mantle, a royal welcome home after seven months' absence in India, Japan, Korea, and China. They have in this brotherhood a company of men, some forty in number, who call themselves "The Miracles." Not a man in the company who has not been redeemed from drunkenness, or worse, within the past three years! One of the number had written a welcome song for the occasion, and another had composed the music. I saw those "miracles" stand up, the whole forty of them, and heard them sing that song. Ex-gamblers and prize-fighters, they all joined in the singing, and with a spirit that brought tears to the eyes of the superintendent whom they thus honored, and to the eyes of many other men in that great audience. Talk about a Lazarus! I saw forty Lazaruses that afternoon. Dr. Samuel Chadwick's suggestion, that the getting of a Lazarus will do more than any thing else to start a mighty revival, is worth thinking about.

The hall in Deptford was opened in October, 1903. Not a Sunday has passed since then that they have not had conversions there. Four years ago the only hall was a small room seating about two hundred people; to-day there are four halls, seating five thousand. Central Hall is the largest, and has a seating capacity for two thousand. The membership has grown in three years from one hundred and ninety to over two thousand. Three years ago there was one minister, one lay evangelist, no deaconesses, and no bandmen. To-day there are four ministers, six lay evangelists, twelve deaconesses, and four bands with a hundred and twenty-five bandmen. The bandmen are all enthusiastic Christian men, all total abstainers, and all nonsmokers. This mission reaches large numbers of dockers and stevedores. The social side of the work is simply astonishing, particularly the work for the poor boys and girls. Some of the boys were in the Sunday afternoon service, and they seemed intensely interested in Mr. Mantle's vivid portrayals of the things he saw in India and China.

MISSION IN KINGSWAY

The West London Mission, since the death of Hugh Price Hughes, has not been flourish-

—REV. J. E. RATTENBURY

ing; it has been on the decline. This does not seem to be the fault of the workers. First, Saint James's Hall was sold; then the mission was removed to Exeter Hall, an exceedingly bad location for the purposes of the mission. After long debate and much wrangling the chapel in Great Queen Street was turned over to the uses of the mission. A considerable amount of money was expended in fitting it up. At the last Conference Rev. J. E. Rattenbury, of illustrious Methodist ancestry and a man who successfully conducted a mission at Nottingham, was appointed superintendent. Plans are under way to enlarge the auditorium, add clubrooms, and provide a great entrance from Kingsway—a fine new street recently cut straight through from Oxford Street to the Strand.

Mr. Rattenbury is an interesting and magnetic speaker. His oratory is not of the conventional type, but rather of the sort which made Arius the Libyan so powerful and persuasive a pulpit orator. I heard him on Sunday evening in the first of the six sermons he has been preaching on social topics. It was the only mission I visited or heard of where the evangelistic appeal was not made in the Sunday night service. Some of Mr. Rattenbury's friends rather apologized for him next day by saying that he was bidding for his audience, being new in the mission, and that after he had his audience he would be as evangelistic as any of the missioners. Let us hope so. But there are some who will doubt the wisdom of a preacher trying to *get* an audience by preaching socialism, or any other *ism*, with the expectation that he will *hold* that same audience by preaching the saving power of Jesus Christ. I had read in the British Weekly the day before an interview with Mr. Rattenbury on "Why I am a Socialist." Socialism is the one great and absorbing topic in England just now. Of course, what Rattenbury and men like him mean by declaring themselves to be socialists is not that they are political but Christian socialists. They are trying to show that the good in socialism, rightly understood, is a part of the program of Christianity.

SOUTH SIDE MISSION

The last hall I visited was the one superintended by Rev. Henry T. Meakin. It is located in a deserted and dirty part of South London, about a mile east of Spurgeon's Tabernacle. No more interesting work is to

CENTRAL HALL, SOUTH LONDON MISSION

be seen anywhere. The mission was founded eighteen years ago. Mr. Meakin, formerly in the railroad service, was superintendent when the new hall was building, and has seen the prosperity of the work from the opening until now. The present membership is about fifteen hundred and steadily increasing. It is estimated that fully seven thousand people, young and old, pass through the hall every week. The most characteristic feature of the work here is what is done for the children. Plans are on to do more. Mr. Meakin has a considerable amount pledged for a great institutional building for children, to be located just across the street from Central Hall. He has a theory that the cheapest, quickest, and most effectual way in which to improve the slum community is to care for the neglected children. "I would have," says he, "a state record for, and oversight over, every individual child until the child has passed through the preparatory period of life and has emerged into an age of responsibility for itself." He says further: "At all costs there should be no out-of-works between the ages of thirteen and eighteen." When the home of which Superintendent Meakin is dreaming is built, and the twenty-five hundred children are actually there, it will be a place worth going to see.

"THE OLD ORDER CHANGETH"

It was in 1891 that I got my first glimpse of the Wesleyan Church. During the summer of that year I attended the Conference, which was held at Nottingham. There I heard many of the leading men on the floor of the Conference and in services held in the chapels of the city. Later I visited many chapels in London and other cities. The impression made was not favorable. It seemed to me that the Wesleyans of England were in a rut, and that, with the exception of a few noble and notable men, the more earnest spirit of Methodism had departed. The Methodism I saw seemed little less than an imitation, and a poor imitation at that, of the Established Church, having no fine, strong, vigorous, independent life and power of its own. Perhaps I had expected too much. Perhaps I did not see all I ought to have seen. But the impression made was as I have described it. I am coming back home from this visit, sixteen years later, amazed and thrilled by what I have seen. The mission halls had few advocates sixteen years ago. To-day their spirit is pervading the whole Wesleyan Church. It

REV. HENRY T. MEAKIN

is hardly too much to say that these halls have transformed the Wesleyan Church. Peter Thompson said to me: "If it had not been for the mission halls, we shouldn't have had the Million Guinea Fund, and if we hadn't had the Million Guinea Fund, Methodism to-day would be depressed, if not disheartened." I have talked with leading representatives of the Methodist press, with distinguished ministers in circuits as well as in mission halls, with professors in three of the Wesleyan theological colleges, with members of the editorial staff of great papers both religious and secular, with eminent professors and ministers outside of the Wesleyan Church, with business men as well as clergymen, with students as well as professors, and the testimony, in every case, has been an expression of deep appreciation of what the mission halls have done and are doing, not only for the Wesleyan Church, but for Christianity and for the social betterment of the waste places in the cities of England. The Wesleyan Church is overwhelmingly committed to the mission-hall idea. On the strength of testimony received I am safe in saying that the mission halls never had the confidence of the Methodists of England as they have to-day. And there is

be made helpful in the great business of saving men."

MISSION HALLS IN AMERICA

To what extent the mission hall may be adopted to advantage here in America I do not pretend to say. Others who have given more careful study to the problem of the American city will be better able to judge. I can think just now, however, of at least three districts in as many of our large cities where I should like to see the experiment tried. Perhaps we should do well to use another name. The typical mission hall with us is such a cheap affair that few would understand what we meant. Whatever we may think of transplanting the method, there can be no doubt that the *spirit* of the mission hall, which is preëminently and persistently evangelistic, is needed here as well as in England. In every mission I saw, with the possible exception of West London, the fire of evangelism is burning brightly. It is a sane evangelism, too. It says to the unsaved man: "Jesus Christ wants you. He died for you. If you let him, he will make out of you the man you ought to be. Come!" It says to the redeemed man: "Bring yourself to your best; be as strong and fully developed as it is possible for you to be. Win

somebody else; be Christ's messenger to someone who is now where you were. Render
some social service—brighten a home, help a
boy, stand against the things that hurt, lend
a hand; remember, you are Christ's man, and
as Christ's man you are, like him, to go about
doing good." The watchword everywhere in
the mission halls seems to be, *"Evangelism and
Social Service."*

I should feel condemned if I did not add a
word of confession, and say that my visit to
these twelve missions has been an inspiration
to my own soul. I went on this trip for a rest
and recreation. I found both, though in a manner I did not anticipate. In looking into the
work of these mission halls, I have read new
chapters in the Acts of the Apostles, and have
seen such visions of opportunity that I am
coming back determined, God helping me, to
put more emphasis on evangelism and to render
more worthy social service. I am deeply indebted to my brethren across the sea for much
kindness shown and many delightful cour-
tesies which shall not be forgotten; but my
great obligation to them grows out of the
privilege they gave me of seeing the work
they are doing for the social and spiritual
regeneration of England.

CPSIA information can be obtained at www.ICGtesting.com
Printed in the USA
BVOW06s1304110816

458707BV00018B/102/P

9 781331 871323